3/13

A Note

D0628702

DK READERS is a compellin
readers, designed in conjuncti
experts, including Dr. Linda C
Professor of Education at Clemson University. Dr. Gambrell has served as President of the National Reading Conference, the College Reading Association, and the International Reading Association.

Beautiful illustrations and superb full-color photographs combine with engaging, easy-to-read stories to offer a fresh approach to each subject in the series. Each DK READER is guaranteed to capture a child's interest while developing his or her reading skills, general knowledge, and love of reading.

The five levels of DK READERS are aimed at different reading abilities, enabling you to choose the books that are exactly right for your child:

Pre-level 1: Learning to read
Level 1: Beginning to read
Level 2: Beginning to read alone
Level 3: Reading alone
Level 4: Proficient readers

The "normal" age at which a child begins to read can be anywhere from three to eight years old. Adult participation through the lower levels is very helpful for providing encouragement, discussing storylines, and sounding out unfamiliar words.

No matter which level you select, you can be sure that you are helping your child learn to read, then read to learn!

LONDON, NEW YORK, MUNICH,
MELBOURNE, AND DELHI

Managing Editor Laura Gilbert
Design Manager Maxine Pedliham
Publishing Manager Julie Ferris
Art Director Ron Stobbart
Publishing Director Simon Beecroft
Pre-Production Producer Marc Staples
Senior Producer Shabana Shakir
Jacket Designer Satvir Sihota

Designed and edited by Tall Tree Ltd
Designers Richard Horsford and
Malcolm Parchment
Editor Catherine Saunders

Reading Consultant Linda B. Gambrell, Ph.D.

For Lucasfilm
Executive Editor J. W. Rinzler
Art Director Troy Alders
Keeper of the Holocron Leland Chee
Director of Publishing Carol Roeder

First American Edition, 2013
10 9 8 7 6 5 4 3 2 1
Published in the United States by DK Publishing
375 Hudson Street, New York, New York 10014

Copyright © 2013 Lucasfilm Ltd. and ™
All Rights Reserved. Used Under Authorization
Page design copyright © Dorling Kindersley Limited

001–187421–Apr/13

All rights reserved under International and Pan-American Copyright Conventions. No part of this publication may be reproduced, stored in a retrieval system, or transmitted in any form or by any means, electronic, mechanical, photocopying, recording, or otherwise, without the prior written permission of the copyright owner.
Published in Great Britain by Dorling Kindersley Limited

DK books are available at special discounts when purchased in bulk for sales promotions, premiums, fund-raising, or educational use.
For details, contact:
DK Publishing Special Markets
375 Hudson Street, New York, New York 10014
SpecialSales@dk.com

A catalog record for this book is available
from the Library of Congress.

ISBN: 978-1-4654-1017-7 (paperback)
ISBN: 978-1-4654-1018-4 (hardback)

Color reproduction by Alta Image
Printed and bound in China by L.Rex

Discover more at
www.dk.com
www.starwars.com

Contents

4 What is a bounty hunter?
6 Jango Fett
8 In action
10 Zam Wesell
12 Code of honor
14 Boba Fett
16 Jabba the Hutt
18 Dangerous job
20 Darth Vader
22 Bossk
24 Teaming up
26 Aurra Sing
28 Princess Leia
30 A deadly job
32 Quiz

DK READERS

BEGINNING 2 TO READ ALONE

STAR WARS®

BOUNTY HUNTERS FOR HIRE

Written by
Catherine Saunders

ALLEN COUNTY PUBLIC LIBRARY

What is a bounty hunter?

A bounty hunter is far worse than most other galactic rogues, such as smugglers or pirates. Smugglers transport goods or people around illegally, while pirates steal spaceships.

Smugglers

A crime lord and an evil Sith have hired bounty hunters to find these smugglers, Han Solo and Chewbacca.

Bounty hunters are much more dangerous. A bounty hunter's job is to catch a special kind of prey—people. He or she will capture or even destroy anyone for a special fee, which is called a bounty.

Let's find out about all the most dangerous bounty hunters in the galaxy.

Jango Fett

Meet one of the best bounty hunters in the galaxy. Jango Fett is strong, tough, and cunning. First he carefully tracks his prey, then he captures them. He is also a skilled fighter, which is useful if his prey does not want to surrender.

Every soldier looks, thinks, and fights exactly like Jango Fett.

Jango Fett is so tough that he was chosen to be the template for an enormous clone army. Every soldier is a clone, or copy, of the feared bounty hunter.

Jetpack
Jango carries many deadly weapons. His jetpack enables him to fly short distances. It is armed with three missiles.

In action

A bounty hunter must do whatever it takes to complete his or her mission. For Jango Fett that means fighting Jedi Knight Obi-Wan Kenobi.

Jango Fett is a tough fighter, but Obi-Wan is no ordinary opponent. Fett will need all his secret weapons in this battle.

Obi-Wan is skilled with the Jedi weapon, known as a lightsaber.

The bounty hunter uses his blasters, his flame thrower, and his jetpack, but Obi-Wan will not be beaten. Finally, Fett distracts the Jedi Knight just long enough to escape.

Zam Wesell

Bounty hunters don't take sides—they'll work for whoever pays them the most money. Clawdite bounty hunter Zam Wesell is sent to destroy a politician named Senator Amidala. If Zam succeeds, it could lead to war.

Zam Wesell looks human, but she isn't.

However, Zam isn't concerned about the fate of the galaxy, or its people. Destroying a galactic senator is simply a job to her. Bounty hunters like Zam don't care who has hired them and they rarely ask why.

This is Zam's true appearance. She is a Clawdite shapeshifter.

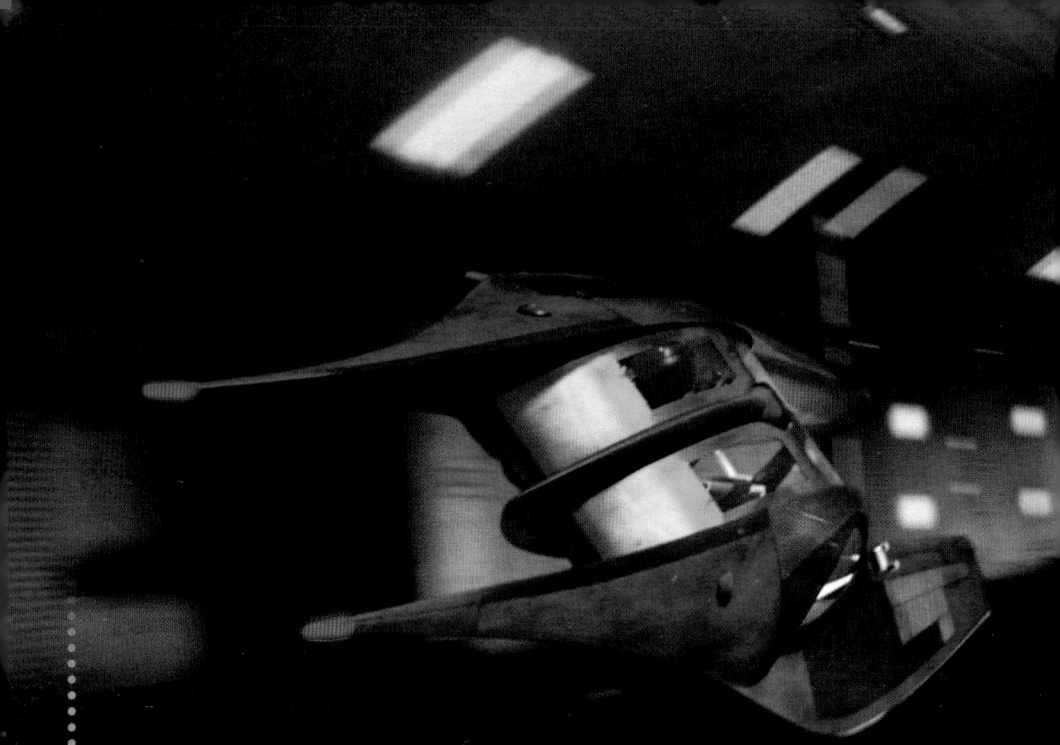

Code of honor

Bounty hunters have an honor code called the Bounty Hunter's Creed. It states that they should destroy only when necessary and that they should never attack another hunter. Some bounty hunters, however, follow the creed only when it suits them.

Zam jumps in her airspeeder to flee from the Jedi, but they catch her.

Zam fails to eliminate Senator Amidala. Instead she is pursued by two Jedi Knights, so Jango Fett eliminates her.

Airspeeder
Zam Wesell pilots a Koro-2 exodrive airspeeder. It is perfect for making speedy getaways.

Boba Fett

This is the most famous bounty hunter in the galaxy—and one of the deadliest. His name is Boba Fett and he is a cunning tracker, an expert marksman, and a determined fighter. Boba is the son of another bounty hunter, Jango Fett.

Boba Fett is actually a clone of Jango Fett, but Jango raised him as a son.

If Boba sets out to track and capture someone, he usually succeeds. He has been on many dangerous missions and his armor bears the scars of many fierce battles.

Slave I

This ship first belonged to Jango Fett. Boba added an ion cannon and a miniature tractor-beam projector.

Jabba the Hutt

Often evil creatures prefer to do business with bounty hunters. Jabba the Hutt is a huge, slimy gangster who lives on the desert planet Tatooine. He is rich, powerful, and very cruel.

Han owes Jabba credits after a smuggling job went wrong.

Jabba lives in a palace and runs a vast criminal empire. He is greedy but very lazy. Jabba uses bounty hunters to do the jobs that he would rather not do himself. He hires Boba Fett to find the smuggler Han Solo, who owes him credits.

Dangerous job

Bounty hunting is a dangerous business. If a bounty hunter is on your trail, he will probably find you. Sometimes, however, in a battle to capture his or her prey, a bounty hunter might lose...

Greedo works for Jabba the Hutt.

Rodian bounty hunter Greedo wants to claim the bounty for Han Solo, so he confronts the smuggler in a busy cantina. Greedo pulls out his blaster, but Han Solo reacts quicker. He wins a deadly shoot-out and escapes.

Darth Vader

Evil Sith Lord Darth Vader rules the galaxy with Emperor Palpatine. Vader wants to find Han Solo's ship, the *Millennium Falcon*, so he gathers together six deadly bounty hunters.

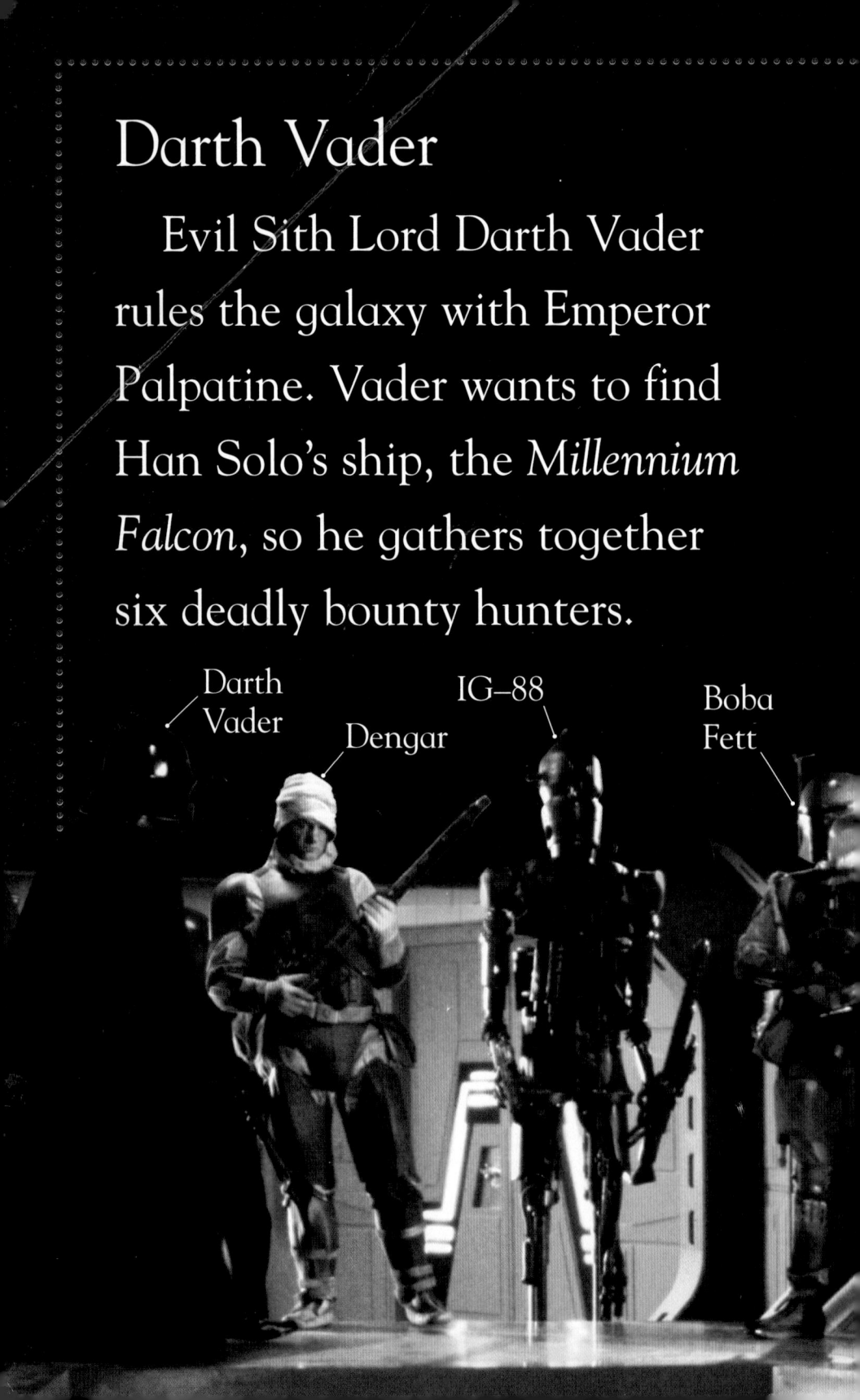

IG–88

This deadly droid is armed and dangerous. He is programmed to search and destroy.

Whoever finds the ship first will receive the bounty. Each bounty hunter is determined to win.

Bossk

4–LOM

Zuckuss

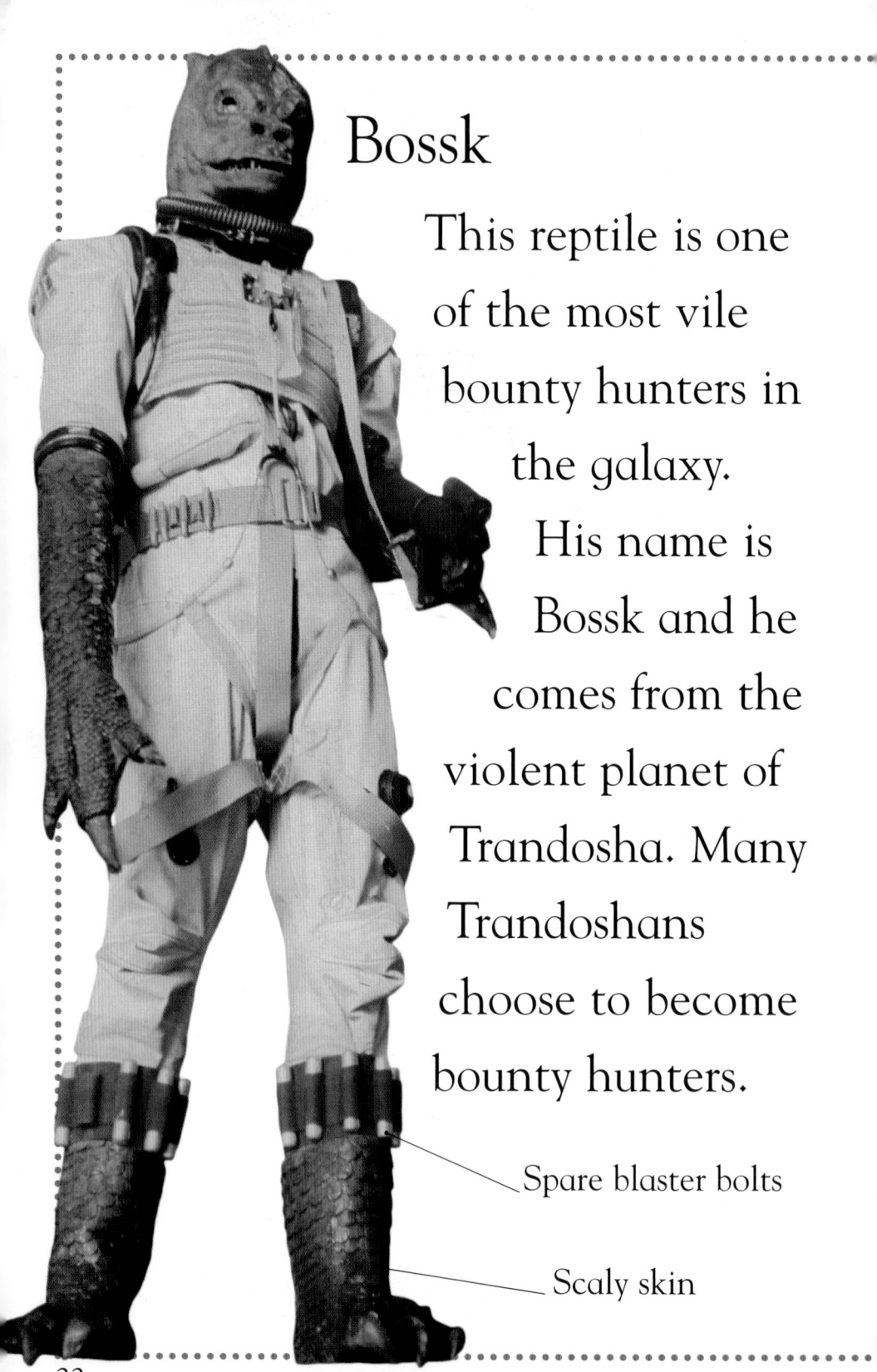

Bossk

This reptile is one of the most vile bounty hunters in the galaxy. His name is Bossk and he comes from the violent planet of Trandosha. Many Trandoshans choose to become bounty hunters.

Bossk and Boba Fett are bitter rivals. Each one believes he is the better bounty hunter.

Bossk's specialty is hunting Wookiees. Only the fiercest bounty hunter can hunt Wookiees as they are over 2 meters (6 feet 6 inches) tall and extremely strong. The vicious Bossk is currently on the trail of the smuggler Han Solo and his Wookiee co-pilot Chewbacca. He is determined to find them before Boba Fett does.

Jango Fett gives Zam Wesell her orders.

Teaming up

Most bounty hunters prefer to work alone. However, for some missions they need to team up. Jango Fett and Zam Wesell joined forces to try and eliminate Senator Amidala, while 4-LOM and Zuckuss often work together.

In fact, 4–LOM and Zuckuss work better as a team. The droid 4-LOM is highly intelligent, while the insectoid Zuckuss is able to use the powerful Force to track prey.

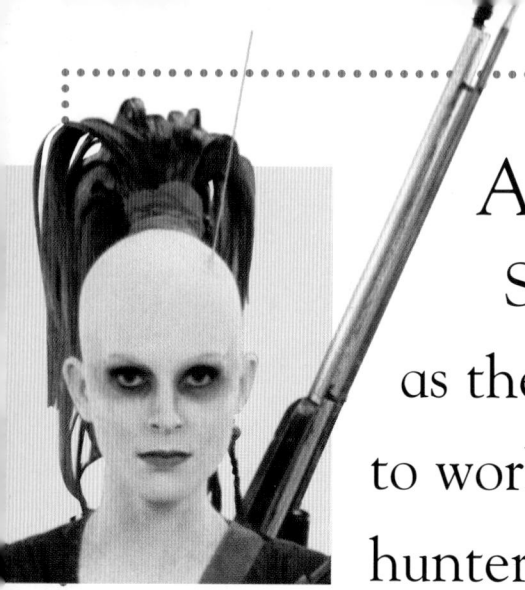

Aurra Sing

Some people, such as the Jedi, don't like to work with bounty hunters. The Jedi believe in honor and justice, but bounty hunters work for whoever pays them. It is rumored, though, that bounty hunter Aurra Sing used to be a Jedi.

Mentor

After the death of Jango Fett, Aurra Sing guided young Boba Fett. She taught him how to be a successful bounty hunter.

No one knows if the rumors are true, but Aurra Sing certainly despises the Jedi. She is a cold-blooded tracker who uses many different deadly weapons. These include blasters, a rifle, and a red lightsaber.

Aurra Sing is ruthless and specializes in tracking Jedi.

Princess Leia

Not every bounty hunter is exactly what they seem. This bounty hunter is rebel leader Princess Leia, in disguise.

Rebel princess

Leia is one of the leaders of the Rebel Alliance. The rebels want to restore freedom to the people of the galaxy.

Leia is wearing the clothes of a dead bounty hunter, Boushh, in order to rescue Han Solo from Jabba the Hutt. Unlike a regular bounty hunter, Leia is not being paid by anyone. She is risking her life to save her friend.

Leia succeeds in her mission to rescue Han.

A deadly job

Being a bounty hunter is a very dangerous job. Bounty hunters track, capture, and often fight with other people. They usually work alone. Life as a bounty hunter can be hard.

Jango Fett was a great bounty hunter, but his job cost him his life.

Bounty hunters have to be tough and be prepared to risk their lives to complete their missions. They often work for very bad individuals, such as Jabba the Hutt or Darth Vader, and hunt very good individuals, such as Han Solo. Generally things don't end very well for bounty hunters...

Jango Fett was not tough enough to defeat Jedi Master Mace Windu.

Quiz

1. Is Han Solo a pirate?

2. Where is Greedo from?

3. Who lives in a palace on Tatooine?

4. Who likes to hunt Wookiees?

5. Who is disguised as Boushh?

6. Can a droid be a bounty hunter?

Answers: 1. No, he is a smuggler. 2. Rodia 3. Jabba the Hutt 4. Bossk 5. Princess Leia 6. Yes, just ask 4-LOM and IG-88.